THE
HORSE
BOOK

Horses of Historical Distinction

Shire Publications, an imprint of Osprey Publishing Ltd
c/o Bloomsbury Publishing Plc, PO Box 883, Oxford,
OX1 9PL, UK
Or
c/o Bloomsbury Publishing Inc., 1385 Broadway, 5th
Floor, New York, NY 10018, USA
E-mail: shire@shirebooks.co.uk

www.shirebooks.co.uk

SHIRE is a trademark of Osprey Publishing Ltd, a
division of Bloomsbury Publishing Plc.

First published in Great Britain in 2017

A CIP catalogue record for this book is available from
the British Library.

ISBN: HB: 978 1 78442 227 1
ePub: 978 1 78442 226 4
ePDF: 978 1 78442 225 7
XML: 978 1 78442 224 0

17 18 19 20 21   10 9 8 7 6 5 4 3 2 1

Typeset in Goudy Oldstyle and Gill Sans

Printed in China through World Print Ltd.

Front cover image:
Mambrino by George Stubbs, 1799.
(Bridgeman Images)

Back cover image:
Mares and Foals Without a Background by George
Stubbs, c.1762. (Bridgeman Images)

Half-title image:
A French mail coach, 1865. (John Paul Getty
Museum)

Shire Publications supports the Woodland Trust, the
UK's leading woodland conservation charity. Between
2014 and 2018 our donations are being spent on their
Centenary Woods project in the UK.

THE
HORSE BOOK

Horses of Historical Distinction

Kathleen Walker-Meikle

INTRODUCTION

The fates of people and horses have been entwined for thousands of years. First hunted as a source of food, the horse (*Equus ferus caballus*) was then domesticated around six thousand years ago, and since then, has played an enormous role in human civilisation. Horses have ploughed fields, raced on tracks, pulled chariots, carts and carriages, and have been used as mounts for travel and cavalry use. They have been carefully bred for different purposes, so we have breeds from the mighty Shire horse, standing at around 17 hands (173cm to the withers), to the diminutive Fallabella (no more than 8 hands, around 80cm at the withers).

Since the invention of steam and internal combustion engines, the horse's central role in transportation has greatly diminished in many countries, as trains, lorries, planes and cars have taken their place in moving people and cargo from one place to the other. The horse still plays an important part around the world, particularly as a working animal in agriculture, helping to herd livestock, move heavy loads, plough fields and even thresh grain. It is now often ridden for pleasure, from enjoyable hacks in the countryside to participating in equine sports such as dressage, eventing, show-jumping or barrel-racing. Watching (and betting) on horses racing against each other is enjoyed by millions of people around the world.

This little book presents a short introduction to horses in history. Horses abound in mythology and literature, from the chariot-mad son in Aristophanes' *The Clouds* to the appropriate steeds of both Don Quixote and Sancho Panza. Poets have written verses praising their qualities. Horses have played a fundamental part in warfare for millennia, from pulling chariots to hauling artillery pieces and cavalry charging en masse. They have also been used for entertainment in circuses, specialist horse shows, films, television series and have even been trained to perform 'mathematical' tricks for an audience. Horses have always been beloved by their owners, and this book recounts some of these partnerships from the Ancient Roman emperor Caligula's doted-on equine Incitatus, to Copenhagen, the Duke of Wellington's loyal steed in battle. And horses have been an inspiration to artists and craftsman, from cave-paintings of wild horses to proud portraits immortalising records of racing champions.

The Przewalski's Horse (*Equus ferus przewalskii*) is the last surviving subspecies of true wild horses, as opposed to feral horses, which are domesticated horses (*Equus ferus caballus*) or their offspring (such as the Brumbies of Australia or the Mustangs of the American West). The Przewalski's Horse became extinct in the wild but is now being reintroduced in small numbers in Mongolia and China. The species is named after the nineteenth-century Russian explorer Nikolai Mikhailovich Przhevalsky, who described the rare horse in 1881. They are dun-coloured, often with stripes on the legs, and live in small family groups.

There are also wild animals of the wider equid family, such as zebras, onagers and wild asses.

Horses abound in Ancient Greek mythology and literature. Pluto, God of the Underworld, drove a chariot pulled by four black or sky-coloured horses. Their names were Abatos ('inacessible'), Abaster ('lacking light'), Aeton ('swift as an eagle') and Alastor ('avenging spirit'). Helios, the Sun-God, used a variety of horses to pull his sun-chariot across the sky; they included Aethon, Amethea, Eous, Phlegon and Pyrois. His son Phaeton attempted to drive the chariot across the sky but could not control the horses, and damaged the earth below by the erratic motion of the chariot. Zeus, King of the Gods, sent a thunderbolt, which destroyed the chariot, sent the horses flying back to their stable and plunged Phaeton fatally to earth.

Other mythical horses included the Mares of Diomedes, King of Thrace. Their names were Podargos ('swift'), Lampon ('shining'), Xanthos ('yellow') and Deinos ('terrible'). They were wild and had a reputation for eating people. The Greek hero Hercules killed their owner and fed Diomedes to his own horses. This diet calmed them down and Hercules was able to bring them back to King Eurystheus as one of his Labours.

A twelfth-century game piece showing Hercules feeding Diomedes to his own horses.

Horses appear in Homer's *Iliad*. The Trojan hero Hector is referred to as the 'breaker of horses'. Balios ('dappled') and Xanthos ('blonde') pulled the chariot of the fabled Achaean warrior Achilles. They were immortal horses, a gift to Achilles' father Peleus, on the occasion of his wedding, who gave them in turn to his son. They could run as fast as the wind and when Achilles' beloved comrade-in-arms, Patrocles, was killed in battle while driving them, they wept:

> *They were unwilling to go back to the wide passage of Helle and the ships, or back into the fighting after the Achaeans, but still as stands a grave monument which is set over the mounded tomb of a dead man or lady, they stood there holding motionless in its place the fair-wrought chariot, leaning their heads along the ground, and warm tears were running earthward from underneath the lids of the mourning horses who longed for their charioteer, while their bright manes were made dirty as they streamed down either side of the yoke from under the yoke pad.*

Iliad, Book XVII

Xanthos was given the power of speech by the goddess Hera and prophesied Achilles' death, but was soon struck dumb by the Furies.

A terracotta krater showing a chariot, c.1300–1230 BC.

Pegasus was the famous winged horse of Greek mythology, who brought thunderbolts to Zeus, King of the Gods. Water gushed up in every place where Pegasus struck the ground with his hooves. The hero Bellerophon was advised to find the horse in order to kill the chimera, a monster with a lion's head, a goat's body and serpent's tail. Bellerophon found Pegasus drinking at a spring, and in some versions of the story, caught him with the help of a golden bridle provided by Athena, Goddess of Wisdom.

Riding on Pegasus, Bellerophon was able to fly to the chimera's lair and kill it with his spear. Unfortunately, despite being a mortal, Bellerophon was filled with hubris and attempted to fly up to Mount Olympus, the home of the gods. This angered Zeus, who sent a gadfly to bite Pegasus. The horse bucked Bellerophon, who fell to earth.

Only in much later versions of the myth is Pegasus ridden by the hero Theseus, in order to destroy a sea-monster with the head of Medusa and thus rescue the princess Andromeda. In earlier versions he merely flies with the aid of Hermes' winged sandals.

A volute-lamp showing Pegasus, first century AD.

Another winged horse was Arion, who could speak and had feet instead of hooves, and pulled the chariot of Poseidon, God of the Sea. Other mythological horse-like creatures included centaurs, unicorns and hippogriffs. Centaurs consisted of the top half of a man and the bottom half of a horse; hippogriffs had the top half of an eagle and the bottom half of a horse.

In Ancient Greek and Roman literature, unicorns were treated not as mythological beasts, but as real creatures, which lived in India. A second-century text, the *Physiologus*, includes an allegory about the unicorn, in which it could only be tamed by a young maiden (representing the Virgin Mary). This formed the basis of the unicorn of medieval romance, symbol of chaste love. Marco Polo talks about seeing unicorns on his journey to Cathay, but from his description of them (hair like a buffalo, feet like an elephant, face like a boar, and ugly), he appears to be describing the rhinoceros.

Unicorn horns were considered to have great value in the medieval and early modern period, as it was believed that they could detect the presence of poison. Extant ones are the tusks of narwhals.

A fifteenth-century aquamanile in the shape of a unicorn.

Bucephalus was the beloved horse of the Macedonian general and conqueror Alexander the Great (356–323 BC). As a young teenager, Alexander tamed the Thessalian horse, which no one had previously been able to do. He did this by noticing that the horse was afraid of its shadow, so turned the animal into the sunlight so it could not see it. The horse's name means 'ox head' – a reference to a branding mark on its haunch that resembled one. Bucephalus was black, and is described as having a star on his forehead. Alexander rode the horse in all his conquests. Bucephalus was once kidnapped, and in his rage, Alexander threatened to destroy the entire region; the horse was returned promptly. Bucephalus died at the grand age of thirty, either from old age or from battle-wounds, in 326 BC. Alexander buried him in a tomb and named a city in the Punjab (Bucephala) in his honour.

A fifteenth-century depiction of Alexander taming Bucephalus.

It is time perhaps to give directions, in case one has to deal with a horse that is too spirited or too sluggish, for the correct way of managing either. First, then, it must be realised that spirit in a horse is precisely what anger is in a man. Therefore, just as you are least likely to make a man angry if you neither say nor do anything disagreeable to him, so he who abstains from annoying a spirited horse is least likely to rouse his anger. Accordingly, at the moment of mounting, the rider should take care to worry him as little as possible; and when he is mounted, he should let him stand still longer than is otherwise usual, and then direct him to go by the most gentle aids. Then let him begin at a very slow pace and increase the speed with the same gentle help, so that the horse will not be aware of the transition to a quicker motion.

Xenophon, On Horsemanship, 350 BC

A black-figure calyx-krater, early fourth century AD.

The frustration of parents towards spendthrift horse-mad children is illustrated in Aristophanes' comedy *The Clouds*, 419 BC.

STREPSIADES: ... oh! misery, it's vain to think of sleep with all these expenses, this stable, these debts, which are devouring me, thanks to this fine cavalier, who only knows how to look after his long locks, to show himself off in his chariot and to dream of horses!? ... Why did I borrow these? Ah! I know! It was to buy that thoroughbred, which cost me so much. How I should have prized the stone that had blinded him!

PHIDIPPIDES (asleep): That's not fair, Philo! Drive your chariot straight, I say.

STREPSIADES: This is what is destroying me. He raves about horses, even in his sleep.

PHIDIPPIDES (asleep): How many times round the track is the race for the chariots of war?

STREPSIADES: It's your own father you are driving to death ... to ruin. Come! what debt comes next, after that of Pasias? ... Three minae to Amynias for a chariot and its two wheels.

PHIDIPPIDES (asleep): Give the horse a good roll in the dust and lead him home.

Virgil's *Georgics* gives characteristics of a good horse in 29 BC:

See from the first yon high-bred colt afield,
His lofty step, his limbs' elastic tread:
Dauntless he leads the herd, still first to try
The threatening flood, or brave the unknown bridge,
By no vain noise affrighted; lofty-necked,
With clean-cut head, short belly, and stout back;
His sprightly breast exuberant with brawn.
Chestnut and grey are good; the worst-hued white
And sorrel. Then lo! if arms are clashed afar,
Bide still he cannot: ears stiffen and limbs quake;
His nostrils snort and roll out wreaths of fire.
Dense is his mane, that when uplifted falls
On his right shoulder; betwixt either loin
The spine runs double; his earth-dinting hoof
Rings with the ponderous beat of solid horn.

A Roman charioteer holding a victor's palm, second or third century AD.

In the *Shahnameh*, the tenth-century Persian epic by the poet Ferdowsi, the hero Rustum rides Rakhsh, a beautiful dappled stallion with a black mane and tail. They have many adventures together. Rakhsh means 'lightning' and the horse would not allow anybody apart from Rustum to ride him. His owner described the magnificent steed as follows:

> *Its body was a wonder to behold,*
> *Like saffron petals, mottled red and gold;*
> *Brave as a lion, a camel for its height,*
> *An elephant in massive strength and might.*

Raksh Saves Rustam from a Lioness, c.1500.

According to the Greek historian Herodotus, Darius I, King of Persia, gained his throne with the assistance of a neighing horse. Herodotus recounts that after the assassination of the usurper Gaumata, seven Persian nobles debated the future of the Persian Empire. One suggested a republic, another an oligarchy, while Darius, one of the seven, argued for a monarchy. They agreed on a monarchy, and decided to choose the king by the following method: six of the nobles would assemble on horseback at sunrise, and he whose horse neighed first would become king. Just before dawn, Darius' groom Oebares rubbed his hands over a mare and then placed his hands in front of the nostrils of Darius' horse as the nobles were gathered. The stallion neighed in excitement and Darius became king.

Relief of Syrians with horses, Persepolis, Iran, dating from around the reign of Darius I.

Horses appear frequently in Chinese mythology. The seventh animal in the twelve-year zodiac cycle is the horse. One reason for the swift horse's low ranking is that all of the zodiacal animals raced across a river, in order to determine the zodiac order. The Snake crossed the river by wrapping itself around the Horse's hoof, and frightened it as it reached the bank, so the Horse was delayed.

The logma is a horse with wings and dragon scales. The tenth-century *Taiping Imperial Reader* claims that a logma appeared in 741 as a good omen for Emperor Xuanzong:

> *It was spotted blue and red, and covered with scales. Its mane resembled that of a dragon, and its neighing was like the tone of a flute. It could cover three hundred miles. Its mother was a common horse which had become pregnant by drinking water from a river in which it was bathed.*

Horse and willow tree, Chinese, fifteenth century.

Incitatus was a horse belonging to the mad Roman emperor Gaius Caesar, better known as Caligula, who was assassinated by his own Praetorian Guard. According to two Roman historians:

He used to send his soldiers on the day before the games and order silence in the neighbourhood, to prevent the horse Incitatus from being disturbed. Besides a stall of marble, a manger of ivory, purple blankets and a collar of precious stones, he even gave this horse a house, a troop of slaves and furniture, for the more elegant entertainment of the guests invited in his name; and it is also said that he planned to make him consul.

Suetonius, *The Twelve Caesars*

One of the horses, which he named Incitatus, he used to invite to dinner, where he would offer him golden barley and drink his health in wine from golden goblets; he swore by the animal's life and fortune and even promised to appoint him consul, a promise that he would certainly have carried out if he had lived longer.

Cassius Dio, *Roman History*

A circus charioteer from the Villa dei Severi at Baccano, third century AD.

As soon as a foal is born, it is possible to judge its natural qualities immediately. If it is good-humoured, if it is courageous, if it is not alarmed by the sight or sound of something new; if it runs in front of the herd, if it surpasses its age-mates in playfulness and eagerness on various occasions and in racing, if it leaps over a ditch and crosses a bridge or a river without baulking – these are the signs of generous mettle.

Columella, *De Re Rustica*, first century AD.

The Ancient Romans adored chariot races, which were held in hippodromes, where fans cheered on their favourite teams: the Blues, the Whites, the Greens and the Reds.

Now the spring races are on; the praetor's dropped his napkin and sits there in state but those horses just about cost him the shirt off his back one way or another; and if I may say so without offence to that countless mob, all Rome is in the Circus today. The roar that assails my eardrums means, I am pretty sure, that the Greens have won, otherwise you'd see such gloomy faces, such sheer astonishment as greeted the Cannae disaster after our Consuls had bitten the dust. The races are fine for young men; they can cheer their fancy and bet at long odds and sit with some smart little girl friend, but I'd rather let my wrinkled old skin soak up this mild spring sunshine than sweat all day in a toga.

Juvenal, *Satires* XI, late first to early second century AD.

Third-century Roman mosaic depicting a chariot race.

In Norse mythology, the horses Alsviðr ('very quick') and Árvakr ('early awake') pull the sun across the sky.

Skinfaxi and Hrímfaxi are the horses of Dagr and Nótt, the personifications of day and night.

The goddess Gná rode Hófvarpnir ('hoof-kicker'), a flying horse, on behalf of Odin's wife, the goddess Frigg.

Odin, king of the gods, rides Sleipnir, an eight-legged horse. One of his descendants is the very swift horse, Grani, ridden by the hero Sigurd. The shield-maiden Brunhild rides on Vingskornir. In one of the sagas, King Heithrek is asked the following riddle: 'What runs on ten feet, has three eyes, but only one tail?' Heithrek correctly answers that it is Odin riding Sleipnir.

Ninth-century depiction of one of the Viking sagas, Isle of Gotland.

The horses of the Irish mythological hero Cú Chulainn are
described thus:

*Two steeds of like size, beauty, fierceness, and speed, bounding together
… high-headed, spirited, powerful, pricking their ears, thin-mouthed,
with long tresses, with broad foreheads, much speckled, slightly slender,
very broad, impetuous, with curling manes, with curling tails. At the
right pole of the chariot is a grey horse, broad-haunched, fierce, swift,
fleet, wild, taking small bounds, broad-maned… thundering, stamping,
with curling mane, high-headed, broad-chested … there darts from him
a flash of breath, a blast of red-sparkling fire stands out from his curbed
jaws. The other horse jet-black, hard-headed, round, slender-footed,
broad-hoofed … spirited, curly, plaited, tressed, broad-backed, firmly
shod … fiery, fierce, strongly striding, firmly stamping, long-maned,
curly-maned, long-tailed, with firm curls, broad of forehead, beautiful
he moves along after having beaten the horses in the land, he bounds
over the smooth dry sward, he follows the levels of the midglen, he finds
no obstacle in the land.*

The Wooing of Emer by Cú Chulainn (author unknown)

The Roman historian Tacitus in his *Germania* (c.98 AD) claimed that the German tribes sought to know the future from horses:

It is peculiar to this people to seek omens and monitions from horses. Kept at the public expense, in these same woods and groves, are white horses, pure from the taint of earthly labour; these are yoked to a sacred car, and accompanied by the priest and the king, or chief of the tribe, who note their neighings and snortings. No species of augury is more trusted, not only by the people and by the nobility, but also by the priests, who regard themselves as the ministers of the gods, and the horses as acquainted with their will.

The feverish horse ought to be treated with a warm bath, and in winter it ought to be warmed so that it does not shiver, and a little feed of vetch-seeds or wheat flour should be given, and warm water should be offered to drink, and the entire body ought to be anointed with wine and warm oil, and the belly ought to be purged, and blood ought to be let from the neck or from the veins around the throat or the chest or from those of the foot.

Geoponica XVI, a tenth-century Byzantine compilation of horse lore

Fragment of a slip-decorated bowl with a horse and rider, thirteenth century.

The Anglo-Saxons were noted for fighting on foot, a fact remarked on by the sixth-century Byzantine historian Procopius in his book *The History of the Wars*. However, he clearly errs in his belief that Britain is completely devoid of horses.

These islanders are the most valiant of the barbarians with whom we are acquainted, and they fight on foot. For not only do they not know how to ride, but it is their lot not even to know what a horse is like, since in this island they do not see a horse, even in a picture, for this animal seems never to have existed in Britain. But if at any time it should happen that some of them, either on an embassy, or for some other reason, should be living with Romans or Franks, or with anyone else that has horses, and it should be necessary for them to ride on horseback, they are unable to mount, but other men have to help them up and set them on their horses' backs....

Hywel Dda, the tenth-century Welsh king of Deheubarth, codified the status, price and fine for damaging horses in medieval Welsh law:

Whoever shall borrow a horse and chafe its back badly so that much hair falls off, four pence are to be paid to the owner. If, however, the back swells from the chafing of an old sore, and the skin be broken to the flesh, eight pence are to be paid. If there be no old sore on it, and the skin and flesh be cut to the bone, sixteen pence are to be paid. Whoever shall deny the killing stealthily of a stallion or palfrey [riding horse], let him give the oaths of twenty-four men…. Whoever shall ride a horse without consent of the owner, let him pay four pence for mounting, and four for alighting, and four for every rhandir [subdivision of land] which he traverses, to the owner of the horse; and a fine of three cows to the king.

Horses could be commandeered by royal messengers in medieval England. Below is a patent of 1396 on payments for hiring horses for messengers between Dover and London:

The king therefore ordains by this patent that there shall be taken for the hire of a hakenei from Southwark to Rochester 12d; from Rochester to Canterbury 12d; Canterbury to Dover 6d; and from town to town according to the rate of 12d. and the number of miles; that the petitioners be in no wise compelled to let their horses for hire unless paid promptly and that for better security of the horses a branding iron be kept in each of those towns by an approved person for branding without payment horses on hire.

The system was open to abuse, as an Act of 1397 legislated imprisonment for 'people of evill condition which, of their own authority take and cause to be taken royally horses and other things … saying and devising that they be to ride on hasty messages and business, where of truth, they be in no wise privy to any business or messages'.

A thirteenth-century ivory chess piece in the form of a queen on a horse.

Horses be joyful in fields, and smell battles, and be comforted with noise of trumpets to battle and to fighting; and be excited to run with noise that they know, and be sorry when they be overcome, and glad when they have the mastery. And so feeleth and knoweth their enemies in battle so far forth that they arese on their enemies with biting and smiting, and also some know their own lords, and forget mildness, if their lords be overcome: and some horses suffer no man to ride on their backs, but only their own lords. And many horses weep when their lords be dead. And it is said that horses weep for sorrow, right as a man doth, and so the kind of horse and of man is medlied.

Bartholomaeus Anglicus, *De proprietatibus rerum*, thirteenth century

Detail from The Adoration of the Magi, *by Bartolli di Fredi, c.1390.*

Rodrigo Díaz de Vivar, known as El Cid, was a twelfth-century Castilian military leader, whose exploits were immortalised in the epic poem *El Cantar de mio Cid*. The poem gives him a great horse named Babeica ('fool' or 'dullard'), who makes an appearance after the siege of Valencia. The slightly earlier Latin poem *Carmen Campidoctoris* mentions an unnamed North African horse of great speed and ability, which was purchased for a thousand dinars by El Cid.

The *Leyenda de Cardeña*, a collection of legendary texts on El Cid composed in the thirteenth century, claims that when El Cid died, his wife put his corpse, sitting up and tied to a saddle, on Babeica so that his enemies would think he was still alive. The *Leyenda* then claims that Babeica died two years later in the same monastery where the texts were composed, at the grand age of forty, having never been ridden since the death of his famous master.

William FitzStephen described London's Smithfield in
the twelfth century:

*Outside one of the gates there, immediately in the suburb, is a certain
field, smooth (Smith) field in fact and name. Every Friday, unless it
be a higher day of appointed solemnity, there is in it a famous show of
noble horses for sale. Earls, barons, knights, and many citizens who
are in town, come to see or buy. It is pleasant to see the steppers in
quick trot going gently up and down, their feet on each side alternately
rising and falling. On this side are the horses most fit for esquires,
moving with harder pace yet swiftly, that lift and set down together, as
it were, the opposite fore and hind feet; on that side colts of fine breed
who, not yet well used to the bit. In that part are the sumpter horses,
powerful and spirited; here costly chargers, elegant of form, noble of
stature, with ears quickly tremulous, necks lifted, haunches plump.
In their stepping the buyers first try for the gentler, then the quicker
pace, which is by the fore and the hind feet moving in pairs together....
In another part of the field stand by themselves the goods proper to
rustics, implements of husbandry, swine with long flanks, cows with
full udders, oxen of bulk immense, and woolly flocks. There stand the
mares fit for plough, dray, and cart, some big with foal, and others with
their young colts closely following.*

Old Smithfield Market, *by Jacques-Laurent Agasse, 1824.*

51

Wie ryter der kunge herre Josaphat mit
synen dienern spacieren vnd die meister ouch
vnd sicht in man vor im eins blinden der and'

In the Arthurian romance *Sir Gawain and the Green Knight*, the Green Knight comes to Camelot riding a green horse. The horse's mane and tail is knotted and tied with gold thread: 'both were bound about with a band of bright green set with many a precious stone; then they were tied aloft in a cunning knot, whereon rang many bells of burnished gold.' After presenting the challenge, horse and rider gallop off, and sparks fly from the horse's hooves.

Gawain in turn rides his steed Gringalet. The saddle is decorated with gold fringes, and the bridle with gold buttons, so they gleam in the sunlight. Gawain greatly cares for his horse:

Then was Gringalet ready, that was great and strong, and had been well cared for and tended in every wise; in fair condition was that proud steed, and fit for a journey.

Fifteenth-century depiction of Josaphat meeting a blind man.

The Venetian traveller Marco Polo described the Chinese city of Chengdu in the thirteenth century:

You must know that the Khan keeps an immense stud of white horses and mares; in fact more than 10,000 of them, and all pure white without a speck. The milk of these mares is drunk by himself and his family, and by none else, except by those of one great tribe that have also the privilege of drinking it. This privilege was granted them by Chinghis Kaan, on account of a certain victory that they helped him to win long ago. The name of the tribe is Horiad. Now when these mares are passing across the country, and any one falls in with them, be he the greatest lord in the land, he must not presume to pass until the mares have gone by; he must either tarry where he is, or go a half-day's journey round if need so be, so as not to come nigh them; for they are to be treated with the greatest respect.

Medieval Chinese depiction of a mongol with horse and camel.

Bayard was a magical bay horse in medieval French *chansons de geste*. In the *Quatre fils Aymon*, the horse can carry the hero Renaud de Montauban and his three brothers all at once. Renaud has to give his horse to Charlemagne, who has a stone tied to Bayard's neck, who is then pushed into a river. But the horse escapes to safety. Bayard became a generic name for a bay horse and by the late Middle Ages in English literature they are rather foolish and blind animals, seen in a line in Chaucer's *Canterbury Tales*: 'Ye been as boold as is Bayard the blynde. That blondreth forth and peril casteth noon'.

'Stand, Bayard, stand!' The steed obeyed
With arching neck, and bended head,
And glaring eye, and quivering ear,
As if he loved his lord to hear.

Sir Walter Scott, *The Lady of the Lake*, 1810

In the early fourteenth-century French romance *Le Roman de Fauvel*, a horse named Fauvel resides in the royal palace thanks to the ministrations of Dame Fortune. The term 'fauvel' refers to a pale brown horse and is also used in the poem as an acronym for the following vices: *Flaterie* (Flattery), *Avarice* (Avarice), *Vilanie* (Villainy), *Varieté* (Variability), *Envie* (Envy) and *Lascheté* (Laxity). The satirical poem has ecclesiastical and secular dignitaries travelling from far and wide to the royal place in order to groom Fauvel. The brushing and cleaning with curry-combs of the horse is the origin of the English phrase 'to curry favour' (from the earlier 'curry fauvel').

Just part of the Dauphin's bombastic speech praising his horse the night before the battle of Agincourt in William Shakespeare's *Henry V* (Act 3, Scene 7):

DAUPHIN: *What a long night is this! I will not change my horse with any that treads but on four pasterns. Ca, ha! he bounds from the earth, as if his entrails were hairs; le cheval volant, the Pegasus, chez les narines de feu! When I bestride him, I soar, I am a hawk: he trots the air; the earth sings when he touches it; the basest horn of his hoof is more musical than the pipe of Hermes.*

ORLEANS: *He's of the colour of the nutmeg.*

DAUPHIN: *And of the heat of the ginger. It is a beast for Perseus: he is pure air and fire; and the dull elements of earth and water never appear in him, but only in Patient stillness while his rider mounts him: he is indeed a horse; and all other jades you may call beasts.*

CONSTABLE: *Indeed, my lord, it is a most absolute and excellent horse.*

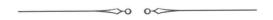

A fifteenth-century depiction of the battle of Agincourt.

Horseshoes were not used in the Ancient World, although there were Roman attempts to use a solid-bottomed iron shoe ('hipposandal'), which was strapped on for bad weather. Nailed-on horseshoes made their appearance in the Early Middle Ages. By the thirteenth century, horseshoes were manufactured in bulk and sold to be nailed onto a horse's feet. 'Hot-shoeing' was not widespread until the sixteenth century.

In medieval England and France, the farrier was called the *mareschal* or marshal. In royal households the marshal was in charge of all of the horses, alongside his other military responsibilities, and the post was one of the most senior offices of the household. The marshal had assistants, and would not need to do the shoeing himself. By the fifteenth century, the title and occupation were separated. The office of Earl Marshal of England survives to this day, held by the Dukes of Norfolk.

In Geoffrey Chaucer's *Canterbury Tales*, each character rode a different kind of horse, very often symbolic of their own nature. The Knight's 'hors were goode' and was a large specimen, as befitted a man of high rank. The proud Merchant rode 'hye on horse', while the Clerk's horse was skinny ('as leane as any rake'). The Shipman rode 'a rouncy as he couth' (an ordinary working horse; the Shipman was clearly not a great horseman), while the Reeve 'sat upon a fit good stot that was all pomely gray, and highte Scot' (a very good horse that was dappled and named Scot). The Wife of Bath 'upon an amblere esily she sat' (an ambler was a pacing horse) and she wore spurs ('And on hir feet a paire of spores sharpe'), while the impoverished plowman rode a mare. They all assembled at a hostelry in Southwark before riding out to Canterbury.

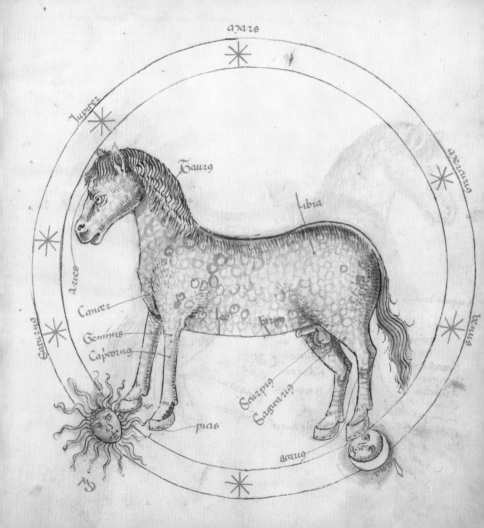

In the Middle Ages, Galenic humoreal theory (which stated that to achieve health one needed to balance the four humours in the body: black bile, yellow or red bile, blood, and phlegm) and medical astrology (where planets and stars were believed to influence the body) were applied to veterinary medicine. Blood-letting was a commonly used technique to restore 'balance' if a horse was ill.

The zodiac horse is an image that replicates a similar popular iconographic scheme for humans. It was used by veterinary practitioners to judge when and when not to bleed a horse. The sky was divided into twelve sections, each ruled by one of the twelve signs of the zodiac. When the moon was in a particular zodiac, the horse was not to be bled in the part of the body ruled by that zodiac sign. For example, if the moon was in Aries, the horse's head should not be bled, if the moon was in Pisces, the hooves should not be bled, and similarly, if the moon was in Cancer, the area around the shoulders should not be bled.

Dame Juliana Berner's *Boke of St Albans* (1486) lists fifteen properties of any good horse, with an animal or human analogy for each:

The. ii. propertyes of a bauson [badger]: The fyrste is, to haue a whyte rase or a ball in the foreheed, the seconde, to haue a whyte fote.
The. ix. propertyes of an hare: The fyrste is styffe eared, the seconde, to haue greate eyen, the thyrde, rounde eyen, the fourthe, to haue a leane heed, the. v. to haue leane knees, the syxte, to be wyght on foote, the. vii. to turne upon a lyttell grounde, the viii. to haue shorte buttockes, the. ix. to haue two good fyllettes.
The. x. properties of a woman: The fyrst is, to be mery of chere, the seconde, to be well paced, the thyrde, to haue a brode foreheed, the fourth, to haue brode buttockes, the fyfthe, to be harde of warde, the syxte, to be easye to lepe uppon, the. vii to be good at a longe iourneye. the. viii. to be well sturrynge under a man, the. ix. to be alwaye besye with the mouthe, the tenth, euer to be chowynge on the brydell.

O young Lochinvar is come out of the west,
Through all the wide Border his steed was the best;
And save his good broadsword he weapons had none,
He rode all unarm'd, and he rode all alone.
So faithful in love, and so dauntless in war,
There never was knight like the young Lochinvar.

He staid not for brake, and he stopp'd not for stone,
He swam the Eske river where ford there was none;
But ere he alighted at Netherby gate,
The bride had consented, the gallant came late:
For a laggard in love, and a dastard in war,
Was to wed the fair Ellen of brave Lochinvar.

Sir Walter Scott, Marmion, Canto V, XII (1808)

St George and the Dragon, *oil on panel by Raphael, c.1506.*

yeq̄ tla ti tetzavitl
yn mal ques.

When the Spanish conquistador Hernán Cortés visited Tayasal of the Itza Maya Kingdom, he left a horse there that had gone lame. After Cortés left, the Itza were unsure of how to feed it, considered the animal a deity, and called it *Tzimin Chac* (Thunder horse). They fed it chicken, fruit, and flowers, but the horse soon died thanks to this inappropriate diet. The Itza made a stone idol of the horse, and worshipped it to demonstrate that they were not responsible for its demise. Some years later the stone idol was destroyed in a fury by a visiting missionary, Juan de Orbita.

Marocco was a famous performing horse in sixteenth-century England. His owner, Thomas Bankes, trained the horse to perform tricks such dancing on hind legs, 'answering' questions with a nod or shake of his head, urinating on command, stomping with his hooves to indicate the amount of coins in a person's purse, spotting the difference between an Englishman and a Spaniard (for the latter he would bare his teeth and whinny), as contemporary poet Thomas Bastard noted:

Bankes hath a horse of wondrous qualitie
For he can fight, and pisse, and daunce, and lie,
And finde your purse, and tell what coyne ye haue:
But Bankes, who taught your horse to smel a knaue?

Bankes and Marocco travelled with the act throughout England, Scotland and even to Paris (where 'Monsieur Moraco' was hugely popular). In France, Bankes had to fend off accusations of witchcraft, and confessed that Marocco was trained to recognise hand gestures.

As if the dead the living should exceed;
So did this horse excel a common one
In shape, in courage, colour, pace and bone.
Round-hoof'd, short-jointed, fetlocks shag and long,
Broad breast, full eye, small head and nostril wide,
High crest, short ears, straight legs and passing strong,
Thin mane, thick tail, broad buttock, tender hide:
Look, what a horse should have he did not lack,
Save a proud rider on so proud a back.

William Shakespeare, *Venus and Adonis*, II

The Small Horse, *by Albrecht Dürer, 1505.*

In Miguel Cervantes' *Don Quixote* (published in two volumes in 1605 and 1615), the eponymous *hidalgo* rides a horse called Rocinante ('whose bones stuck out like the corners of a Spanish Real'). The name means 'formerly a nag'. For Quixote, the name signified what the horse had been, and what it was now (*'antes y primero de todos los rocines del mundo'*: 'the first and foremost of all the nags in the world'). Quixote took time to select the name: 'Four days were spent in thinking what name to give him, because (as he said to himself) it was not right that a horse belonging to a knight so famous, and one with such merits of his own, should be without some distinctive name.' Like his owner, Rocinante is worn out but faithful.

His squire, Sancho Panza, rides a donkey described as *'el rucio'* (dappled). The donkey is sketched thus by his rider: 'he cannot gallop in the air; but, on the king's highway, he shall pace you with the best ambler that ever went on four legs.'

Don Quixote and Sancho Panza, *by Honoré Daumier.*

On the death of Queen Elizabeth I in 1603, Sir Robert Carey galloped to Edinburgh as fast as possible the moment the old queen expired on 24 March, in his eagerness to convey the news to James VI of Scotland. He covered the distance from London to Edinburgh (about 400 miles) in under 60 hours, arriving there on 26 March. By nightfall of the first day he had already covered 160 miles, although he had at least one bad fall on the journey.

James (I of England and VI of Scotland) must have been delighted at the news, as he made Carey a Gentleman of the Bedchamber. However, when the new king arrived in London, Carey was dismissed from his post, due to public disapproval 'for his action contrary to all decency, good manners and respect'. But by 1605 he had regained favour and was named Governor to Prince Charles (later Charles I, who made Carey Earl of Monmouth on his accession).

A Man Mounting a Horse, *attributed to Anthony van Dyck, c.1630.*

'How They Brought the Good News from Ghent to Aix' by Robert
Browning, 1845.

I sprang to the stirrup, and Joris, and he;
I galloped, Dirck galloped, we galloped all three;
'Good speed!' cried the watch, as the gate-bolts undrew;
'Speed!' echoed the wall to us galloping through;
Behind shut the postern, the lights sank to rest,
And into the midnight we galloped abreast.

Not a word to each other; we kept the great pace
Neck by neck, stride by stride, never changing our place
I turned in my saddle and made its girths tight,
Then shortened each stirrup, and set the pique right,
Rebuckled the cheek-strap, chained slacker the bit,
Nor galloped less steadily Roland a whit.

'Twas the moonset at starting; but while we drew near
Lokeren, the cocks crew and twilight dawned clear;
At Boom, a great yellow start came out to see;
At Düffield, 'twas morning as plain as could be;
And from Mecheln church-steeple we heard the half-chime,
So, Joris broke silence with, 'Yet there is time!'

At Aershot, up leaped of a sudden the sun,
And against him the cattle stood black every one,
To stare through the mist at us galloping past,
And I saw my stout galloper Roland at last,
With resolute shoulders, each butting away
The haze, as some bluff river headland its spray:

And his low head and crest, just one sharp ear bent back
For my voice, and the other pricked out on his track;
And one eye's black intelligence, – ever that glance
O'er its white edge at me, his own master, askance!
And the thick heavy spume-flakes which aye and anon
His fierce lips shook upwards in galloping on.

By Hasselt, Dirck groaned; and cried Joris, 'Stay spur!
Your Roos galloped bravely, the fault's not in her,
We'll remember at Aix' – for one heard the quick wheeze
Of her chest, saw the stretched neck and staggering knees,
And sunk tail, and horrible heave of the flank,
As down on her haunches she shuddered and sank.

So, we were left galloping, Joris and I,
Past Looz and past Tongres, no cloud in the sky;
The broad sun above laughed a pitiless laugh,
'Neath our feet broke the brittle bright stubble like chaff;
Till over by Dalhem a dome-spire sprang white,
And 'Gallop,' gasped Joris, 'for Aix is in sight!'

'How they'll greet us!' – and all in a moment his roan
Rolled neck and croup over, lay dead as a stone;
And there was my Roland to bear the whole weight
Of the news which alone could save Aix from her fate,
With his nostrils like pits full of blood to the brim,
And with circles of red for his eye-sockets' rim.

Then I cast loose my buffcoat, each holster let fall,
Shook off both my jack-boots, let go belt and all,
Stood up in the stirrup, leaned, patted his ear,
Called my Roland his pet-name, my horse without peer;
Clapped my hands, laughed and sang, any noise, bad or good,
Till at length into Aix Roland galloped and stood.

And all I remember is, – friends flocking round
As I sat with his head 'twixt my knees on the ground;
And no voice but was praising this Roland of mine,
As I poured down his throat our last measure of wine,
Which (the burgesses voted by common consent)
Was no more than his due who brought good news from Ghent.

In 1623, John Taylor wrote a fearsome tirade against the newly introduced coach; he believed that 'no land has endured more trouble and molestation than this has, by the continual rumbling of these upstart four wheeled tortoises'. The coaches are 'cumbersome by their rumbling and rutting, as they are by their standing still, and damming up the streets and lanes, as the Blackfriars, and other diverse places can witness... the streets are so pestered and clogged with them, that neither man, horse, or cart can pass for them.'

Riding in them wasn't much better, according to Taylor:

It is a most uneasy kind of passage in coaches on the paved streets in London wherein men and women are so tossed, tumbled, jumbled, rumbled, and crossing of kennels, dunghills, and uneven-ways, which is enough to put all the guts in their bellies out of joint, to make them have the palsey or megrum, or to cast their gorges with continual rocking and wallowing.

John Taylor, *The world runnes on wheeles: or oddes betwixt carts and coaches* (London 1623)

William Cavendish, later 1st Duke of Newcastle, was one of the most notable horsemen of the seventeenth century. He was a strong proponent of building a strong and trusting relationship with a horse, rather than relying on brute strength as proposed by many other authorities. He railed against masters such Thomas Blundeville, whose approach he summed up thus: 'He would have Us to Strike a Horse with a Cudgel or Rod, between the Ears, and upon the Head; which is Abominable, though he thinks it a Rare Secret. For Cavendish, force just 'Astonishes the Weak Horse ... makes a Furious horse Madd; makes a Resty Horse more Resty ... and Displeases all sorts of Horses.'

The Riding House at Bolsover Castle was built to Cavendish's exact specifications for the perfect training of horses. His influential books were *Méthode et invention nouvelle de dresser les chevaux* (1658) and *A New Method and Extraordinary Invention to Dress Horses and Work them according to Nature* (1667).

Horse racing was extremely popular in Restoration England. Charles II's eldest illegitimate son, James, Duke of Monmouth, rode to victory in several races, riding horses provided by Thomas Wharton, who bred racehorses in Winchendon. In 1682, Monmouth's progresses to garner support were all structured around the racing calendar, and Wharton's horses, particularly a winning gelding, all ran in the Duke's name. In February 1683, Louis XIV of France organised a horse race that gathered racehorses from all over Europe. Wharton's gelding, running as owned by Monmouth, won with ease. After the race, Louis commented that he would give 1,000 pistoles for such a horse. Wharton at once replied that the horse was not for sale at any price, but that he would be happy to give him to the King as a gift. Louis quickly realised that the price was support for Monmouth, and declined.

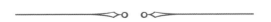

James Scott, Duke of Monmouth at the Siege of Maastricht in 1673, by Jan Wyck.

Problems with false starts sometimes occurred in horse racing, as described by the Earl of Conway in 1682:

Here hapned yesterday a dispute upon the greatest point of Criticall learning that was ever known at Newmarket, A Match between a Horse of Sir Rob: Car's, and a Gelding of Sir Rob: Geeres, for a mile and a halfe only, had engaged all the Courte in many thousand pounds, much depending in so short a course to have them start fairly. Mr Griffin was appointed to start them. When he saw them equall he sayd Goe, and presently he cryed out Stay. One went off, and run through the Course, and claims his money, the other never stird at all. Now possibly you may say that this was not a fayre starting, but the critics say after the word Goe was out of his mouth his commission was determined, and it was illegall for him to say Stay. I suppose there will be Volumes written upon this Subject; 'tis all refered to his Majesty's Judgment, who hath not yet determined it.

The Round Course at Newmarket, Cambridgeshire, Preparing for the King's Plate, by *Peter Tillemans, c. 1725.*

The modern racing Thoroughbred descends from three Arabian stallions of the late seventeenth and early eighteenth centuries.

Byerley Turk was the earliest; he was captured either at the battle of Vienna (1683) or Buda (1686) and brought to England. He served as the horse of Captain Byerley, who rode him in Ireland during the campaigns of William III. When Captain Byerley retired, the horse was put out to stud where he sired many influential horses and mares.

The Darley Arabian was purchased in Aleppo (Syria) in 1704 by Thomas Darley as a gift for his brother. The horse resided as a breeding stallion at Aldby Park.

The final horse, Godolphin Arabian, was born in Yemen in the 1720s and was taken to Tunis, before being sent to France as a gift to Louis XV. The horse was not appreciated in France, however, and was soon purchased by Francis, 2nd Earl of Godolphin. Due to his small stature (15 hands), his role was to act as a 'teaser' for mares in the stud, but he covered a mare (the Lady Roxana) and the pair had three foals, all of which went on to win Godolphin a reputation as a prize stallion. Most Thoroughbreds can be traced back to these three horses.

Various kings have lost their lives while out riding. William II of England was mysteriously shot with an arrow while out hunting in the New Forest. Being mounted on a horse in battle was always risky, as attested by the death of Richard III (battle of Bosworth Field) and James IV of Scotland (battle of Flodden).

William III, King of England and Scotland (and Stadtholder in the Dutch Republic) died in 1702 while out riding his horse Sorrel. As he galloped over the turf, Sorrel stumbled on a molehill, and the king fell to the ground, breaking his collarbone. Complications set in (and pneumonia) and he died shortly after. Jacobites would drink toasts to 'the little gentleman in the black velvet waistcoat', the mole responsible.

Detail from The Farmer's Wife and the Raven, *by George Stubbs, 1786.*

The Prussian King Frederick the Great (1712–1786) was greatly fond of horses. He gave them names of his political contemporaries according their characters, such as Brühl, Choiseul, Kaunitz and Pitt. The horse named Lord Bute was punished in 1762, when Britain stopped financial and military support to Prussia. Lord Bute (the horse, not the first minister) was sent to live in the mules' stables and made to carry out servile duties, in comparison to Frederick's riding horses. When old, the horse Caesar was allowed to meander unhindered through the gardens of the New Palace in Potsdam.

Frederick's favourite horse was named Conde. He never used the horse in battle and only rode him for pleasure. The horse was brought daily to Frederick, who would give him sugar, melons and figs. Conde, if let loose, would quickly find Frederick, and once even followed him into the interior of the Sanssouci Palace. Conde lived to the great age of thirty-eight and his skeleton is still on display in Potsdam.

The eighteenth-century British artist, George Stubbs, is famed for his paintings of horses. In 1756, Stubbs dissected horse carcasses in a barn in Horkstow in Lincolnshire in an attempt to understand the relationship between anatomy and exterior appearance. His sketches became the basis of his book: *The Anatomy of the Horse*, published in 1766.

Most of his commissions were from private patrons, who wanted him to paint their favourite horses. The eighteenth century was a great age for horse breeding and racing, and Stubbs was perfectly placed to immortalise these equines, often with their owners or grooms. One of his patrons, Charles Watson-Wentworth, 2nd Marquess of Rockingham, commissioned the first of Stubbs' famous portraits of horses against plain backgrounds. Rockingham also commissioned the first of Stubbs' series of paintings of horses being attacked by lions. Stubbs continued painting horses, outdoor pursuits and other animals (including the first kangaroo in Western art) until his death in 1806 at the age of eighty-one.

A Lion Attacking a Horse, *by George Stubbs, 1762.*

The French Emperor Napoleon Bonaparte had many horses, ridden in battle and on parades, including Coco, Jaffa, Roitelet, Le Vizer, Marie and Tauris. But his favourite was Marengo, a grey Arabian that he purchased in Egypt 1799 (it was named after his victory at Marengo). He rode Marengo at the battles of Austerlitz, Jena–Auerstedt, Wagram and finally at Waterloo. The horse was found by William, Baron Petre, on the battlefield and was later sold.

In 1823, visitors could pay one shilling (half a shilling for children and servants) to view the famous horse at the Waterloo Rooms in London, complete with his original bridle and saddle, and note the battle scars and the imperial brand with the crown and the letter 'N' on his hindquarters. The newspapers remarked that *'The Horse is so quiet that either Ladies or Children may caress him'*. Marengo died in 1838, and his skeleton is on display at the National Army Museum in Chelsea. One hoof was made into a snuff-box (currently on loan to the Household Cavalry Museum).

Napoleon reviews his troops after the battle of Marengo, *by Baron Antoine Jean Gros, 1802/3.*

Copenhagen was the favourite horse of Arthur Wellesley, Duke of Wellington, who rode him at the battle of Waterloo in 1815. He was bred by General Grosvenor in 1808 and named after the British naval action in Copenhagen. He was raced for a few seasons and then sold to Charles Stewart in 1812, who took him to Spain in the course of the Peninsular War, sold him to another officer who in turn sold him to the Duke of Wellington. When the Duke returned to England, Copenhagen retired to Wellington's estate of Stratfield Saye. He died in 1836, allegedly due to consuming too many 'sponge cakes, bath buns and chocolate creams' (Copenhagen's other habit was his preference for eating lying down) but more likely due to old age. He was buried on the estate in a paddock with full military honours.

The Duke of Wellington said of his horse: 'There may have been many faster horses, no doubt many handsomer, but for bottom and endurance I never saw his fellow.'

A study for a portrait of Wellington on Copenhagen, by Jan Willem Pieneman, 1820 /21.

Marshal Gebhard von Blücher, whose Prussians were decisive at the battle of Waterloo, was not riding his own horse on the day. This was due to his own horse having being shot under him at the battle of Ligny (a French victory) three days before Waterloo. Blücher (aged 72) had led a cavalry counter-attack and was then trapped under his dead horse, as French cuirassiers rode over him at least twice without recognising him, as the marshal played dead. Only at nightfall was a Prussian staff officer able to help him leave the field.

Having your horse killed under you was an occupational hazard for a cavalryman. The French Marshal Ney had four horses shot under him in the course of the battle of Waterloo.

An Episode at the battle of Waterloo, *by William Heath, 1817.*

Traditional fox-hunting, now banned in England, Wales and Scotland, involved tracking foxes on horses with packs of hounds and developed in the eighteenth century due to the lack of suitable game, since deer had become scarce. Each hunt had members with different responsibilities, including the Master of Foxhounds, the Huntsman, the Whippers-In and the Kennelman.

Hunting horses were bred and especially trained for this purpose, as they would have to be able to keep up with the hounds at speed, and jump across numerous obstacles such as hedges and fences in the course of the hunt. The aim was to follow the hounds as they searched for the fox. For many it was an exciting sport, as the poet William Henry Ogilvie described: 'To horse and away To the heart of the fray! Fling care to the Devil for one merry day!'

'The Huntsman's Horse' by William Henry Ogilvie (1869–1963):

The galloping seasons have slackened his pace,
And stone wall and timber have battered his knees
It is many a year since he gave up his place
To live out his life in comparative ease.
No more does he stand with his scarlet and white
Like a statue of marble girth deep in the gorse;
No more does he carry the Horn of Delight
That called us to follow the huntsman's old horse.
How many will pass him and not understand,
As he trots down the road going cramped in his stride,
That he once set the pace to the best in the land
Ere they tightened his curb for a lady to ride!
When the music begins and a right one's away,
When hoof-strokes are thudding like drums on the ground,
The old spirit wakes in the worn-looking grey
And the pride of his youth comes to life at a bound.

He leans on the bit and he lays to his speed,
To the winds of the open his stiffness he throws,
And if spirit were all he'd be up with the lead
Where the horse that supplants him so easily goes.
No double can daunt him, no ditch can deceive,
No bank can beguile him to set a foot wrong,
But the years that have passed him no power can retrieve –
To the swift is their swiftness, their strength to the strong!
To the best of us all comes a day and a day
When the pace of the leaders shall leave us forlorn,
So we'll give him a cheer – the old galloping grey –
As he labours along to the lure of the Horn.

Riders out fox-hunting rode at great speed over many obstacles, and might be reluctant to give up the chase, as exemplified by a young curate out riding with the Duke of Grafton:

The late Duke of Grafton, when hunting, was thrown into a ditch; at the same time a young curate, calling out 'Lie still, my lord', leaped over him and pursued his sport. Such an apparent want of feeling, we may presume, was properly resented. No such thing: on being helped out by his attendant, his grace said, 'That man shall have the first good living that falls to my disposal; had he stopped to have taken care of me, I never would have given him any thing;' having been delighted with an ardour similar to his own, or with a spirit that would not stop to flatter.

The Field Book, 1833

The famed Pony Express ran from April 1860 to October 1861. Mail was sent on individual riders from St Joseph, Missouri, to Sacramento California, via a series of around 157 relay stations. The route was 1,800 miles long and a rider would change his horse at each station, keeping the mail pouch (the *mochila*). Riders would cover around 80–100 miles, and they would ride day and night. The mail would take ten days to arrive. Riders had to be lightweight (no more than 125 pounds) and horses were small, on average around 14½ hands (hence the name Pony Express). The fastest section of the trip was accomplished by Robert Haslam (Pony Bob) in 1861, who rode 120 miles in 8 hours and 20 minutes, carrying President Lincoln's inaugural address. The Pony Express stopped due to the outbreak of the Civil War and the introduction of the electric telegraph.

Horses were used extensively in the US Civil War, for cavalry, artillery and for many logistical purposes. The battle horses of the generals on both sides included Union General Ulysses S. Grant's Cincinnati, Confederate General Thomas Jackson's Old Sorrel and Union General Philip Sheridan's Rienzi (now in the Smithsonian Museum). Traveller was the favourite horse of Confederate General Robert E. Lee, who described him thus to his wife's cousin:

If I was an artist like you, I would draw a true picture of Traveller; representing his fine proportions, muscular figure, deep chest, short back, strong haunches, flat legs, small head, broad forehead, delicate ears, quick eye, small feet, and black mane and tail. Such a picture would inspire a poet, whose genius could then depict his worth, and describe his endurance of toil, hunger, thirst, heat and cold; and the dangers and suffering through which he has passed. He could dilate upon his sagacity and affection, and his invariable response to every wish of his rider. He might even imagine his thoughts through the long night-marches and days of the battle through which he has passed. But I am no artist Markie, and can therefore only say he is a Confederate gray.

Draught horses are usually large horses that were bred for work such as heavy farm tasks or hauling freight. Their use has greatly declined since the invention of the internal combustion engine (particularly cars and tractors). The unit of measurement 'horse power' was invented in the late eighteenth century to compare the output of steam engines with draught horses. Mechanical horsepower, also known as imperial horsepower, was originally defined as a measure of power equal to 550 foot-pounds per second. Early trains, invented in an age dominated by the horse in all aspects of life, were often termed 'iron horses'.

Draught horse breeds include the Shire, Clydesdale and Percheron. The largest horse on record was a Shire called Sampson, foaled in 1846, who stood at 21.2½ hands high (219cm at his withers) and weighed 1,520kg. He was renamed Mammoth at the age of four.

The writer Mark Twain describes a rather uncomfortable journey in the American West in 1861:

Our coach was a swinging and swaying cage of the most sumptuous description – an imposing cradle on wheels. It was drawn by six handsome horses, and by the side of the driver sat the 'conductor,' the legitimate captain of the craft; for it was his business to take charge and care of the mails, baggage, express matter, and passengers. We three were the only passengers this trip. We sat on the back seat, inside. About all the rest of the coach was full of mail bags – for we had three days' delayed mail with us. Almost touching our knees, a perpendicular wall of mail matter rose up to the roof … We changed horses every ten miles, all day long, and fairly flew over the hard, level road. We jumped out and stretched our legs every time the coach stopped, and so the night found us still vivacious and unfatigued … Whenever the stage stopped to change horses, we would wake up, and try to recollect where we were – and succeed – and in a minute or two the stage would be off again, and we likewise. We began to get into country, now, threaded here and there with little streams. These had high, steep banks on each side, and every time we flew down one bank and scrambled up the other, our party inside got mixed sowewhat. First we would all lie down in a pile at the forward end of the stage, nearly in a sitting posture, and in a second we would shoot to the other end and stand on our heads. And we would sprawl and kick, too, and ward off ends and corners of mail-bags that came lumbering over us and about us; and as the dust rose from the tumult, we would all sneeze in chorus, and the majority of us would grumble, and probably say some hasty thing, like: 'Take your elbow out of my ribs! Can't you quit crowding?'

Mark Twain, *Roughing It* (1872)

Mr G.J. Whyte-Melville in *Fraser's Magazine* (1858) discusses the essential role of horses in society:

How many a nervous gentleman confides his fourteen stone of unwieldy solidity to the discretion and forbearance of his cob, a favourite in whom he places implicit reliance, and on whose sobriety of demeanour depends not only the comfort but the personal safety of his rider. How many a timid lady whom no earthly consideration would induce to put her foot in a boat, steps unhesitatingly into her carriage without an instant's misgiving or consideration that the unsoundness of a strap, the misplacement of a buckle, might at any moment produce the most alarming results…. What with cab, omnibus, fly, tax-cart, pony-carriage, and phaeton, there are few people that are not constantly in the habit of confiding their necks and limbs in one way or another to the intelligence and docility of the horse…. We never know the value of anything but by its loss; and perhaps we are so accustomed to the use and abuse of this valuable animal, that we can hardly realize the inconveniences to which we should be subjected if deprived of his services.

The British Parliament passed in 1835 (and later in 1849 and 1879) a Cruelty to Animals Act, which covered offences of abusing and torturing animals. The offences of beating and over-driving in particular covered horses, and by 1869 the Royal Society for the Prevention of Cruelty to Animals noted that the vast majority of convictions under the Act were against horses, particularly those in urban areas.

The RSPCA's periodical *Animal World* in 1870 connected drink to excessive cruelty:

As occurs hundreds of times during the day, a man will stop to have a beer at a public house, the horses, tired and jaded, are perhaps half asleep when he returns. To make a start, he will touch the leading horse smartly with his whip ... and then comes a sudden tug of the chain enough to pull the poor thing's head off; this is a common thing, and no one steps in to speak a word on its behalf.

Advice for lady riders:

Mount, then, from the ground, if you have some one to put you on and some one to hold your horse; or, if the horse will stand without holding, cautioning your escort – if you are not sure of his expertness in such services – to be sure to raise your foot straight up, and to give you warning by counting one, two, so that you may be certain to have the leg straightened before he begins to lift, as otherwise the result may be the reverse of graceful.

When in the saddle, rise in your stirrup, as already suggested, and smooth down your dress, meantime thanking your escort and telling him how well he did it. This smoothing down of the skirt is a good plan to practise frequently, first standing, then at a walk, then at a trot, till you can do it deftly, almost without thought, for there is no telling at what inopportune moment it may become necessary.

T.H. Mead, *Horsemanship for Women* (1887)

Detail from Lord and Lady Twemlow *by William Barraud, 1840s.*

The novel *Black Beauty* was written by Anna Sewell 'to induce kindness, sympathy, and an understanding treatment of horses'. Sewell, who was disabled from a young age, became dependent on horse-drawn transport, and respected the horses that did this work. The book was a strong call against contemporary cruelty to carriage horses. She particularly took against the bearing rein, which forced horses' heads up high into an uncomfortable but fashionable position. The book became an international bestseller when published in 1877.

It is narrated by Black Beauty the horse, whose adventures as a carriage horse form the basis of the novel. Other horses that make an appearance include the cab-horse Captain (an old war-horse who had been ridden in the Charge of the Light Brigade at the battle of Balaclava), a cheerful pony named Merrylegs, and the tragic Ginger, whom Black Beauty last sees as a broken-down cab-horse and then dead in a cart.

Cities in the nineteenth century abounded with private horse-drawn carriages for hire. In 1834 Joseph Hansom designed the two-wheeled hansom cab, which was designed to be fast and pulled by one horse, and with a low centre of gravity to facilitate sharp turns in city traffic.

The two passengers would sit directly behind the large wheels, while the driver would sit behind, on a seat level with the cab's roof. The front of the cab was open, and two folding doors would close in front of the passengers' legs. Cabs also had side windows and usually leather curtains, which could be drawn across if desired. If there were more than two passengers, the services of a four-wheeled carriage (called a 'growler') could be used instead. In Dublin, most of the carriages for hire were 'jaunting cars', which had two back-to-back bench seats facing outwards, and passengers risked getting thrown off at speed around tight corners.

By the end of the century, cities across the world had hansom cabs, from London to Paris, Berlin, St Petersburg and New York. Innovations flourished, such as rubber tyres by the 1880s (bells were needed to warn other traffic due to their quietness) and the first taximeter, which was invented in the 1890s. By the early twentieth century, motorised vehicles had replaced the horse-drawn cabs.

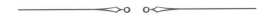

A hansom cab driver gestures at a taxi driver during the taxi strike of 1913.

There were various ways one could call a hansom cab, from shouting to whistling, and you could even buy a special cab-whistle for this express purpose.

In the morning you will send for a hansom, desiring your man to take neither the first nor the second which may present itself. Into this hansom you will jump, and you will drive to the Strand end of the Lowther Arcade, handing the address to the cabman upon a slip of paper, with a request that he will not throw it away. Have your fare ready, and the instant that your cab stops, dash through the Arcade, timing yourself to reach the other side at a quarter-past nine. You will find a small brougham waiting close to the curb, driven by a fellow with a heavy black cloak tipped at the collar with red. Into this you will step, and you will reach Victoria in time for the Continental express.

Sherlock Holmes' advice to Dr Watson in 'The Final Problem'

Big Ben, *1894 by Rose Maynard Barton.*

The late eighteenth and nineteenth century was the age of the *hippodrama*, a wildly popular theatrical entertainment that involved a mix of high drama with circus horsemanship, with titles such as *Marlborough's Heroic Deeds* and *Mazeppa or the Wild Horse of Tartary* (in which the role of the hero tied to a horse was performed by a young lady in a skimpy costume). Ramps were built on stages so the horses could get onstage with ease. But by the mid-nineteenth century their appeal was fading:

Of late years a change has come over the equestrian drama. The circus flourishes, and quadrupeds figure now and then upon the stage, but the 'horse spectacle' has almost vanished. The noble animal is to be seen occasionally on the boards, but he is cast for small parts only, is little better than a four-footed supernumerary.... Plays are not now written for him. He is no longer required to evince the fidelity and devotion of his nature by knocking at street-doors, rescuing a prisoned master, defending oppressed innocence, or dying in the centre of the stage to slow music.

Dutton Cook, A Book of the Play (1876)

In the late nineteenth century Karl Krall claimed that he had trained several horses to do mathematics. The horses were Berto, Hans Kluge, Zarif, Amassis and Muhamed. All apparently could 'read' and do 'basic arithmetic' with the tapping of their hooves. It was attested that Muhamed could even extract the cube root of a number written on a blackboard. He would tap out the ones with his right foot and the tens with his left foot. Contemporaries claimed that they could spot no fraud and that the horses' abilities were genuine, after testing them with sacks over the horses' heads to see if they were being given the answers by Krall.

A similarly trained horse was Clever Hans, who performed such mathematical tricks in early twentieth-century Germany. In 1907, psychologist Oskar Pfungst demonstrated that the horse was not actually doing these 'sums', nor was he being fed the answers by his owner, but that the horse was responding to involuntary cues in the body language of both the owner and the other human observers.

German stunt rider Therese Renz, c.1895.

A passage entitled 'The Riderless War-Horses' from *The Spectator* in 1870, concerning cavalry horses in the Franco-Prussian War:

[Lieutenant-Colonel Pemberton remarked:–] 'Only those who have seen a battle-field can form a notion of the extraordinary way in which the horses, as long as they have a leg to crawl on, will follow the regiment to which they belong. I saw what had evidently been serjeants' horses keeping their position in rear of their squadron, wheeling with it, and halting exactly as if their riders were on their backs, and all the time streaming with blood. Poor creatures! They are indeed to be pitied, for they have neither Vaterland, promotion, nor the coveted medal to think of, whatever maybe the issue; and few indeed are there which have been in action which have not some honourable scars to show.' Again the German Post relates, 'that after the slaughter at Vionville, on the 18th of August, a strange and touching spectacle was presented. On the evening call being sounded by the 1st Regiment of Dragoons of the Guard, 602 riderless horses answered to the summons, jaded, and in many cases, maimed. The noble animals still retained their disciplined habits.'

Charge of the Prussian Cavalry, *by Aime Morot.*

The role of the horse in modern warfare changed during the
First World War.

At the start of the war, cavalry units were considered to be a necessary
part of any army, although their role as an offensive force was reduced
by the use of the machine gun and modern artillery. Nevertheless,
cavalry charges and mounted infantry were used extensively in all
theatres of the war. The newly invented tanks would finally replace the
widespread use of cavalry.

The majority of horses were used for logistical reasons, such as pulling
wagons, ambulances and artillery, and for carrying messages. Horses
were particularly suitable, as unlike mechanical vehicles they were
more likely to be successful over muddy and tough terrain. Millions
of horses were requisitioned from farmers and owners all over Europe
for the war effort.

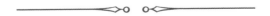

*The author's great-grandfather, George M. Meikle, King Edward's Horse, on Duke. Both horse
and rider survived the war.*

'The Horse That Died For Me' by Trooper Gerardy

They gave me a fiery horse to groom and I rode him on parade
While he plunged and swung for kicking room, like a young and
haughty jade.
I rode him hard till I curbed his will, hot-foot in the sham attack
Till he ceased to jib and took the drill like a first class trooper's hack.
He tasted hell on the Indian sea; pent up in the gloom below,
He dreamed of the days when he was free, and his weary heart beat slow.
But he lived to leave the reeking ship and raised his drooping head
With new-born zest when he felt the grip of earth beneath his tread
I left him and sailed away to fight in the trenches deep –
A stretch that passed like an awful hour of fearsome nightmare sleep
I lived to search for my mount once more on the crowded piquet line:
I rode him out as I did before, when I'd claimed the horse as mine.

[…]

Far out on the hock-deep sands that roll in waves to the flaming sky,
He carried me far on the night patrol where the Turkish outposts lie.
He took me back to the camp at noon when the skirmish died amain,
And under a white and spectral moon he bore me afield again.

[...]

We moved away on the flanking march, like a brown line rudely drawn.
That reached the foot of the grey skies arch in the waking light of dawn.
The line closed in when the red sun shot from the purple-tinted east
To glare with scorn on the wretched lot of man and his jaded beast.
I urged my horse with a purpose grim for a ridge where cover lay,
And my heart beat high for the heart of him when he saved my life that day.
His knees gave way and I slipped from him; he dropped in a sprawling heap
On the wind-gapped edge of the skyline's rim where the high-blown sand
was deep.
And fear came down with a gusty rain of lead on his final bed ...
Before I turned for cover again, I knew that his life had fled.
My heart is warm for a heart that died in the desert flank attack,
And the white sand surges down to the hide and bones of a faithful
trooper's hack.

Trooper Gerardy, Australian light horse ballads and rhymes, 1919

135

In 1925, Swiss-born Aimé Félix Tschiffely set out to ride from Buenos Aires to Washington DC, a distance of nearly 10,000 miles. Tschiffely had only recently learned to ride, but this did not deter him and his quest to prove the value of the Criollo horse. His two horses were Mancha ('Spotty'), a red and white piebald, and Gat ('Cat'), a dun. Both had a tendency to kick and bite anyone who approached. Tschiffely left the Argentine capital, riding with only his equine companions, a .45 Smith & Wesson, a Winchester shotgun, passport, letters of credit, compass, barometer, a poncho, mosquito netting and a hat. They survived raging rivers, mountains, jungles, non-existent trails, the Peruvian Matacaballo ('Horse-killer') Desert, venomous snakes, falling down cliffs, tropical diseases, suspicious border guards, local bandits and other perils, until arriving in Washington, where they received a hero's welcome. They returned by boat to Buenos Aires, and Mancha and Gat retired to an estancia.

The current high-jump record was set in 1949 in Chile by Huaso, ridden by Captain Alberto Larraguibel, and it stands at 2.47 metres (8 feet 1 inch). Huaso was foaled in 1933 and considered quite a failure as a horse: his performance at the racetrack was poor (due to nerves); he suffered a back quarter injury that quickly stopped a dressage career and he did not seem to display much promise as a show-jumper. This changed when an army horse master spotted Huaso bolting and jumping with ease over a 2-metre-high wall. He was purchased by the army and given to Captain Larraguibel to be trained to beat the world record. Huaso was trained for two years and on 5 February 1949 in Viña del Mar, the sixteen-year-old Huaso cleared the 2.47 jump. Afterwards the horse was retired and was not ridden again; he died in 1961.

Horses have appeared in many genres of film from the beginnings of the film industry, in historical films (such as *Ben Hur* and *El Cid*) and even in films about famous horses (such as *Seabiscuit* and *Phar Lap*), but they have been essential to Westerns ever since the first, *The Great Train Robbery* (1903). Many of these early Westerns required the horses to perform stunts that could seriously injure or kill the animals; they were treated as disposable extras. Horses were regularly filmed falling to the ground thanks to trip wires, holes in the ground and other dangerous practices. These reached a head in the filming of *Jesse James* in 1939. To film a scene of a horse plunging over a cliff into water, the horse was put on a slippery platform that tilted so the animal went over the cliff and died. Following public outrage, the American Humane Association was given the right to set safety guidelines and monitor how animals were treated on sets. From 1966 to 1980 due to legal issues the American Humane Association lost some of its rights, but they were reinstated after a horse was killed due to unsafe explosives in the filming of *Heaven's Gate*. Today horses are either trained to fall safely or perform a suitable stunt, although anything too dangerous can be achieved with an animatronic horse.

John Wayne and Dean Martin riding through a western village in a scene from the film
The Sons of Katie Elder, *1965.*

Just like in films, horses have been on television since its early days. *Mister Ed* was an American sitcom that aired from 1961 to 1966. Similar to the popular series of films (seven in total) starring 'Francis the Talking Mule', The plot of *Mister Ed* involved Ed, a talking palomino, his owner Wilbur and the general mishaps that occurred. Part of the humour often involved Mister Ed only talking to his owner – confusion inevitably followed.

Mister Ed wasn't the only famous palomino on TV. Trigger made his name in films (and later several TV series) in the 1940s and 1950s with his owner Roy Rogers. Trigger learned more than a hundred cues for assorted tricks and could walk on his hind legs, sit in a chair, sign his name X, lie down on cue and cover himself with a blanket. Roy Rogers' handprints and Trigger's hoof prints are preserved on the pavement outside Grauman's Chinese Theatre in Hollywood.

Roy Rogers and Trigger.

Horse racing is still hugely popular around the world. Flat racing (on a racecourse without obstacles) is the most common form, with Thoroughbreds being the most popular breed.

National Hunt racing is practised in France, Ireland and the United Kingdom. It involves either jumping over hurdles (made of brush) or over a combination of fences, ditches and water jumps (steeplechase). The most famous National Hunt race is the Grand National at Aintree, a track of over 4 miles with thirty obstacles. Red Rum, a bay Thoroughbred, won the Grand National three times, in 1973, 1974 and 1977. His win in 1973, when he beat Crisp at the final fence having trailed by 15 lengths, is the most famous:

Just a furlong to run now, 200 yards now for Crisp, and Red Rum is still closing on him! Crisp is getting very tired, and Red Rum is pounding after him. Red Rum is the one who's finishing the strongest. He's going to get up! Red Rum is going to win the National. At the line Red Rum has just snatched it from Crisp!

Commentator Peter O'Sullevan on the 1973 race.

Horses jump Bechers Brook during The Topham Steeple Chase at Aintree on 3 April 2009.

FURTHER READING

DiMarco, L.A. *War Horse: A History of the Military Horse and Rider* (Westholme, 2008)

Hyland, A. *Equus: The Horse in the Roman World* (B.T. Batsford Ltd, 1990)

Hyland, A. *The Horse in the Middle Ages* (Sutton, 1999)

Hyland, A. *The Horse in the Ancient World* (Sutton, 2003)

Johns, C. *Horses: History, Myth, Art* (Harvard University Press, 2008)

Kelekna, P. *The Horse in Human History* (Cambridge University Press, 2009)

McCabe, Anne. *A Byzantine Encylopaedia of Horse Medicine* (Oxford University Press, 2007)

Pickeral, T. *The Horse: 30,000 Years of the Horse in Art* (Merrell, 2009)

IMAGES ARE ACKNOWLEDGED AS FOLLOWS:

Author, page 132; Beinecke Rare Book and Manuscript Library, Yale Un iversity, page 62; Bridgeman Images/ Historiska Museet, Stockholm, Sweden, page 37; Bridgeman Images/ Lambeth Palace Library, London, page 58; Bridgeman Images/ Archives Charmet, page 68; Bridgeman Images/ Victoria Art Gallery, Bath and North East Somerset Council, page 84; Bridgeman Images/ Château de Versailles, France, page 96; Bridgeman Images/Barbara Lowe, page 109; Bridgeman Images/ Chris Beetles Ltd, London, page 125; Getty Images, pages 26, 34, 65, 92, 113, 121, 122, 128, 131, 138, 141, 143; John Paul Getty Museum, pages 1, 21, 48, 52, 61; Los Angeles County Museum of Art (LACMA), page 25; The Metropolitan Museum, New York, pages 8, 11, 13, 14, 17, 18, 22, 29, 32, 41, 44, 47, 55, 70, 74, 77; National Gallery of Art, Washington, page 66; Rijksmuseum, Amsterdam, page 98; Wikimedia Commons/Lawrence, page 6; Wikimedia Commons/Marie-Lan Nguyen, page 30; Wikimedia Commons, page 110; Wikimedia Commons/Library of Congress, page 126; Wikimedia Commons/Museum of Fine Arts, Houston, page 72; Yale Center for British Art, pages 3, 50, 87, 89, 90, 94, 101, 103, 106, 118.